NEVER
TOO
OLD

Eleanor Stern

CONTENTS

FOREWORD
. . . . i

PREFACE
. . . . v

CHAPTER ONE
The Call of God on Our Lives
. . . . 1

CHAPTER TWO
Old Timers in the Bible Who Accomplished Their Dreams
. . . . 11

CHAPTER THREE
Old Timers in Our Day Who Fulfilled Their Dream. . . . 23

CHAPTER FOUR
Fulfilling My Calling—Building Kings Kids Village. . . 31

CHAPTER FIVE
        The Vision Grows. 47

CHAPTER SIX
        Challenge to Fulfill Your Vision
                or Calling. 53

Eleanor Stern

FOREWORD

Honor and enjoy your Creator while you're still young, before the years take their toll and your vigor wanes, before your vision dims and the world blurs and the winter years keep you close to the fire. (Ecclesiastes 12:1-2 MSG)

While these words (and the verses that follow) clearly describe the prevailing view toward the aged, every now and again there are those who come along and defy it in grandiose fashion! Such is the case with Pastor Paul and

Eleanor Stern. It was nearly thirty years ago that I first met Pastor Paul, who laid hands on my wife Amy and me, ministering prophetically over our lives, with two other presbyters, as we were being sent out to plant Nairobi Lighthouse Church in Nairobi, Kenya. Even then, many would have considered this dear man of God to be growing old, yet he and Ms. Eleanor would still traverse numerous places across the globe. And Ms. Eleanor continues to champion that cause to this day.

Abraham Lincoln once said, "In the end, it is not the years in your life that counts—it's the life in your years." How can I forget the life that always came through Pastor Paul's ever optimistic, encouraging words and the "Paul Stern Shuffle" as he preached? Who wouldn't be blessed by Ms. Eleanor's consistent, focused resolve, her endearing laugh, and the choruses that came out of her spirit in both the good and challenging times? One of the special honors bestowed upon my wife and me was the joy of presenting the prayer of dedication the day Ms. Eleanor's orphanage was officially opened, as well as later, to minister the dedication message for the Mary Hensold School, in July 2011—both wonderful stories told in this book.

As quoted above, "Before your vision dims and the world blurs..." (Ecclesiastes. 12:2a)— throughout the course of his life, Pastor Paul never allowed the world to go blurry. Both he and Ms. Eleanor kept, and she continues to keep, a lost and dying world without Christ ever in focus. I have observed their commitment to impact the next generation in the sacrificial giving of themselves, even through their golden years. As you read *Never Too Old*, may you be stirred once more, regardless of your age, to stay the course, fulfilling what God has set His hand upon you to accomplish in His Kingdom and for His glory.

Pastor Don Matheny
Nairobi Lighthouse Church
Nairobi, Kenya

PREFACE

This book was written primarily to encourage people in their retirement years to keep on keeping on with life, realizing that sometimes we can accomplish great things, even though we are past normal working years. Don't give up on any dream you have. It's worth it to press in and do it.

But I also want people to know what a great place Kings Kids Village (KKV) in Nairobi, Kenya is. It took a lot of work, and many people giving their time or money, or both, to build Faith

House, the Banda, the playground and the school. It is producing great young people who love God, love life and are interested in doing great things. It has become well known in Nairobi as a super example of a place to raise orphans. You are welcome to come and visit. If you can't come in person or if you want to learn more, please visit our web site:

www.kingskidsvillage.org

I want to thank my family for their part in helping me complete this book.

Thank you Phil for encouraging and showing me how to get this book published.

Thanks Sue for pushing me and helping me with my computer skills.

Thank you Jon for being so willing to make sure this vision continues by overseeing and caring for KKV.

I thank Steven for having the passion to spread the word about KKV to everyone he knows.

Most of all I thank Paul, my husband, for his support and help to see this vision come to pass. I miss him very much!

Eleanor Stern
May, 2015

Paul and Eleanor Stern

x

CHAPTER ONE

The Call of God on Our Lives

It was a beautiful, clear Sunday morning in Nairobi, Kenya as we drove to City Stadium to attend Sunday service at Nairobi Lighthouse Church. As we made our way to our seats, I looked out over the field where three large white cranes circled in preparation to land. What a beautiful place to attend church... under such a beautiful blue sky. As I opened my Bible to read during the pre-prayer time, a verse on the right side at the top of the page caught my attention. I began to read.

> "Arise, cry out in the night, At the beginning of the watches; Pour out your heart like water before the face of the Lord. Lift your hands toward Him For the life of your young children, Who faint from hunger at the head of every street." (Lamentations 2:19 NKJV)

I looked across the page and there another verse stared me in the face.

> My eyes fail with tears, my heart is troubled; my bile is poured on the ground because of the destruction of the daughter of my people, because the children and the infants faint in the

streets of the city. (Lamentations 2:11 NKJV)

I don't often read Lamentations, but
I knew instantly that it was the Holy
Spirit speaking to me. My first reaction
was, "God, You can't be serious! Paul
and I are seventy-five years old. You
want us to start an orphanage now?"
And just like God, He answered me
with these words:

"You aren't as old as Abraham and
Sarah, and I'm not asking you to give
birth to a natural child."

"Well, thanks for that!" I exclaimed.
After reading those two verses, I told
God that I would pray. And I did.

You may be asking yourself, "What
made her think God was speaking to
her?" Well, let me take you back a few
years, sixty two to be exact. Paul and I
had just married and moved to Detroit,
Michigan to become part of a church
that was experiencing an awesome
revival. During one of the morning

sessions, the pastoral staff was ministering to people with the laying on of hands and prophecy. They called us up to pray for us. Everything they spoke to us that day, about how God wanted to use us, had come to pass except the very last prophetic word given by our pastor. Turning to me, she had said, "You shall be the mother of an orphanage Many shall grow up to become pillars in the house of the Lord."

Morning Devotions

Eighteen months later the church commissioned and sent us to Kenya, where we ministered for three years. Off and on during that time I asked the Lord about starting an orphanage, but there was no indication it was in the picture. In Kenya, at that time, the ex-

4

tended family took care of their orphans.

In 1960 we were again commissioned and sent to Nigeria by the same church, Bethesda Missionary Temple, now called Bethesda Christian Church. During the years we were in Nigeria, building churches, starting a Bible School and training pastors, I would ask the Lord about an orphanage, but He gave me no indication that we were to start one, even though we lived through the Biafran war that took place during that time, which I'm sure resulted in many orphans.

We returned home in 1970 and for three years were on staff at Bethesda. God then called us to move to Danville, Illinois to start a church, which we did in 1973. God moved in an awesome way as He brought many hungry people who helped build The Rock Church. During the fifteen years we pastored there, a beautiful church was built, a school was added, and some seventeen people were sent out from there into full-time ministry. It was a fruitful time, and we loved what God was doing. From time to time I would ask, "Lord, is an orphanage still in the picture?" I really believed the prophetic word that had come to me.

During those years, our son Jonathan and his wife Molly, answered the call of God on their lives for Africa, and we, as The Rock Church, sent them to Kenya. During one of our visits there, Jon introduced us to Pastor Don and Amy Matheny who were building Nairobi Lighthouse Church. Pastor Don asked Paul to be an overseer to him in his work there, which Paul gladly did. These two connections took us to Kenya every few years during the 1980s.

Jon and Molly Stern

Sometimes events in your life change the direction you are going. In 1998 Paul had a heart attack. During his recovery the doctor asked him what he did for a living. Paul told him that he was a pastor but also traveled and ministered in conferences. The doctor told him that he had better give up something, as it was too hard on his heart. After much prayer, he felt it was time to give up pastoring. A few weeks later we were on our way to spend several weeks in Nigeria. On our return trip, we stopped in Germany for two weeks to minister in The Rock Church (Der Fels) in Mainz, Germany, and to be with Pastors Jan and Meis Barendse, founders of the church. While we were there, Pastor Jan invited us to work with him in taking supplies to Eastern Europe, which was just opening up to the West after years of Communism. This we did. Every time we went to Romania and saw the poverty-stricken orphanages, my heart cried out for those babies and children. "God, should we start an orphanage here in Romania?" No answer...just silence.

We lived in Germany and Hungary for almost five years, going back and forth to these Eastern European countries, ministering in their churches and taking food and supplies to the needy. Twice during those years, Pastor Matheny asked us to come to Nairobi and oversee the church so he and his family could come back to the United

States for a couple of months. Then came the day I told you about in the beginning of this chapter.

CHAPTER TWO

Old Timers in the Bible Who Accomplished Their Dreams

Why am I writing about this couple, Paul and Eleanor Stern, being challenged to do something as unusual as beginning an orphanage at the age of seventy-five? Let me ask you this question. What would you do if asked to step out of your comfort zone, sell your house, move to a totally different country and begin an orphanage—at the age of seventy-five? We in America have been programmed to believe that when we reach "old age," it's time to sit back, move to Florida, play golf and just relax. We've worked hard for many years and it's time to take it easy. After all, isn't sixty-five the magic retirement age? Social Security sends us a "retirement" check every month and most people carry a supplemental insurance policy to cover their medical needs, etc. So, why not relax?

Relaxing is not the problem. Thinking I'm old at the age of sixty-five is! Whenever friends used to ask, "Are you going to retire in Florida?" I would answer, "With all those old people?" I was beginning to feel a little old at seventy-five when the Lord challenged me with the needs of the orphans in Africa. As you know, HIV-AIDS has hit Africa with a mighty, destructive force, causing there to be thousands and thousands of children with no parents. Often the orphaned children are left with an old grandmother who can barely care for herself, or, just as often, there is no one to care for the family except the oldest child. When I **FORGOT ABOUT MY AGE AND CONCENTRATED ON THE NEED**, I knew that we had to do something. Later I'll tell you the results, but now, I want to zero in on why we are 'Never Too Old' to keep on keeping on.

Kids at Kings Kids Village

Abraham and Sarah

The Lord mentioned Abraham and Sarah to me that Sunday morning in Nairobi, and I'd like to remind you a little about their lives. In Genesis chapter twelve we read the story of their move from Haran where his father had brought the family from Ur of the Chaldees. Abraham had a direct Word from the Lord:

> The LORD had said to Abram, "Leave your native country, your relatives, and your father's family, and go to the land that I will show you. I will make you into a great nation. I will bless you and make you famous, and you will be a blessing to others. I will bless those who bless you and curse those who treat you with contempt. All the families

on earth will be blessed through you." So Abram departed as the LORD had instructed, and Lot went with him. Abram was seventy-five years old when he left Haran. (Genesis 12:1-4)

That was quite a move to make at that age, even in that day. All his family, friends, and everything familiar to them were to be left behind. They were to go to a place that God would show them. They didn't even know exactly where they would make their home! God blessed them as they settled into their new area, and they became very rich. They had only one problem—no children! They tried on their own to fix that problem in their life, and they had Ishmael—not the "promised son" from God.

Time went on, and soon Abraham turned ninety-nine years old. He didn't know it, but it was time for the promise to be fulfilled. The promise came again:

> But God replied, "No—Sarah, your wife, will give birth to a son for you. You will name him Isaac, and I will confirm my covenant with him and his descendants as an everlasting covenant." (Genesis 17:19)

Later, we read:

> Abraham was 100 years old when Isaac was born. (Genesis 21:5)

Sarah was ninety! That was a total miracle to us, but to God it was just keeping His Word, not even looking at their age.

We make such a big deal about our age, but God looks at what He has planned for us. We might be able to mess up His plans a little by hesitating to do what He has asked us to do, but He will give grace to anyone who really wants to fulfill the call of God for his or her life.

Caleb

Another ordinary person God used in old age was a man named Caleb. God told Moses to send twelve men, one from each tribe, to spy out the land of Canaan and bring back a report. On their return, ten brought back a report of fear and inability to win against the enemy. The other two, Joshua and Caleb, came back enthusiastically saying, "We are well able to go in and possess the land." (Numbers 13:30 Paraphrased) God was displeased with those who ignited all the rest of the people with their fear, so God told Moses that all the men twenty years of age and older would die in the wilderness, not entering into the land of Canaan. Only Joshua and Caleb would have that privilege.

The day came for Israel to enter Canaan. Joshua, who had become their leader, was giving out the land to all the tribes. Caleb came to him and reminded him of the promise God had made to him in Deuteronomy 1:36.

> "So that day Moses solemnly promised me, 'The land of Canaan on which you were just walking will be your grant of land and that of your descendants forever, because you wholeheartedly followed the LORD my God.' Now, as you can see, the LORD has kept me alive and well as he promised for all these forty-five years since Moses made this promise—even while Israel wandered in the wilderness.

Today I am eighty-five
years old. I am as strong
now as I was when Moses
sent me on that journey,
and I can still travel and
fight as well as I could
then." (Joshua 14:9-11)

Caleb was as strong at age eighty-five
as he was at forty. Many of the Old
Testament prophets lived to a ripe old
age, still strong, still doing the will of
God, still encouraging the people. If a
person's health fails and he is not able
to continue doing the same physical
things he was once able to do, then God
will give him or her something that will
fit what he or she is able to do. After my
husband, Paul's, heart attack at the age
of sixty-two, he gave up pastoring the
church but kept right on ministering all
over the world, which led us back to
Kenya.

Job

One more person we read about in the Bible that I would like to bring to your attention is Job. Job was an adult, well thought of in his community and an honest and God-fearing man. God allowed the devil to take everything from him and to strike his body with boils from head to foot. Job was restored after he realized that God was God and didn't need Job to do His work. He just needed an obedient Job to do what God had set before him.

Not only did God restore all Job's animals and wealth, He gave him an increase. God also gave him another ten children; seven sons and three daughters. They grew up to be adults, and we see the beauty of the three daughters mentioned at the end of the book. Job lived more than 140 years after his restoration. Now I know people lived longer in those days, but **THAT** long? Yes! Long enough to be active in busi-

ness, in counseling, and in being a productive father.

Abraham and Sarah— Caleb—
Job— three wonderful examples from
the Bible on staying productive even in
your old age.

CHAPTER THREE

Old Timers in Our Day Who Fulfilled Their Dream

Now let us look at our day. We can find quite a number of people who are very effective in their old age. Some of our Senators and Representatives in Washington have passed the age of sixty-five by quite a few years, and they are still being elected by the people of their state because they are doing a good job.

One evening while I was watching TV, the host of the program was interviewing Art Linkletter. He was in his mid nineties and still had speaking engagements as well as writing books. He was an inspiration to all of us who remember him from years ago when he had the popular TV program called *Kids Say the Darndest Things*.

Another person I would like to tell you about is a wonderful lady in Lincoln, Nebraska named Katherine Dwinell. She lived in an independent living area of a retirement facility, exercised every day for two hours, attended a Bible study every week, and was in church every Sunday morning, right on the front row. When you asked her how she felt, she would simply say, "I'm blessed and highly favored of the Lord." She told me one day that if she said how she really felt, I wouldn't want to hear it, and if she said she is fine, she would be lying. Katherine lived to be 107 years old, still loving and believing in God, who had put her right where she belonged for as long as He wanted her there.

Yet another great example is a pastor from Shippensburg, Pennsylvania named Elvina Miller. She and her husband pastored for many years before he died, after which she carried on alone. She traveled to several countries in West Africa and had a radio program there for many, many years. However, in 1999, at the age of eighty-three, she felt to go to Ghana and open up a training school, whereby young people could be trained in many occupations as well as ministry. She continued to visit the school off and on until just a very few years ago.

Recently someone sent me an email of another story which made my day. It was written by a university student, telling about a fellow student he had met. When their professor told them to turn to someone they didn't know and introduce themselves, he turned around and saw this wrinkled old lady with a big smile on her face.

"Hi, Handsome. My name is Rose and I'm eighty-seven years old. Can I give you a hug?"

That was the beginning of a daily walk after class. When he asked her why she was in college at that ripe old age, she said, "I always dreamed of having a college education and now I'm getting one!"

At the end of the semester, Rose was invited to speak at a football banquet. As she began to speak, she dropped her three by five cards on the floor. A little embarrassed, she leaned into the microphone and simply said, "I'm sorry I'm so jittery. I gave up beer for Lent and this whiskey is killing me! I'll never get my speech back in order so let me just tell you what I know."

As the students laughed, she cleared her throat and began, "We do not stop playing because we are old. We grow old because we stop playing."

Something else that was said by the person who sent the email really grabbed my attention.

"If you are nineteen years old and lie in bed for one full year and don't do one productive thing, you will turn twenty years old. If you are eighty-seven years old and stay in bed for a year and never do anything, you will turn eighty-eight. Anybody can grow older. That doesn't take any talent or ability. The idea is to grow up by always finding opportunity in change."

Elderly folks don't usually regret what they did, but rather what they did not do. By the way, Rose, whose one desire was to go to college, finished her college degree and one week after graduation died peacefully in her sleep. What an example!

My parents, Carl and Emma Ratter, were a great example to me. My father didn't quit his job until he was nearly seventy years old, after which he and my mother decided to go to Brazil for six months to visit relatives who had moved there from Germany many years before. Their sole purpose was to know their spiritual condition and see if they could be a blessing to them. After their six months there, they returned home with both a glad heart and a sad heart, knowing that some of their family did know the Lord but others did not. They later took a trip back to Germany to see the spiritual condition of relatives there. By this time my parents were in their early eighties but still going strong. It was while in Germany that my father had a mild stroke which caused them to hurry home. He lived to be eighty-eight, still praising the Lord and having an active voice in the church.

In her late eighties my mother told me that she didn't sleep very well at night. So, I asked her if she got up or just stayed in bed. She answered that she just lay there and prayed for all her children, for the church, and anyone else God brought to mind. She passed away just three months short of ninety years old. What a heritage I have and what an example!

Before I close this chapter, I would also like to tell you another great benefit Paul and I received by doing God's will whenever He asked anything of us. He blessed us with four wonderful children. All of them are totally productive citizens and serving God in whatever they do. That is some of the rewards we have from being faithful to do what He asked us to do, even in our old age.

Well, it's time to catch you up on what God did and is doing in Nairobi.

CHAPTER FOUR

Fulfilling My Calling— Building Kings Kids Village

A few weeks after my conversation with God in the stadium, we returned to America. I was in prayer daily about what to do. One morning, a couple of months later, the Lord spoke to my heart with these words, "You can't start an orphanage in Kenya while sitting here in America." I knew that was true, but Paul had meetings scheduled all over the States and I knew he couldn't go with me. When I told Paul that I would go to Kenya by myself, he suggested I ask my sister-in-law, Barbara, to go with me. I had not even given a thought as to who would like to go along. When I called Barbara, she said she'd get back to me after talking to her two daughters. Barb is a year older than me and had never been to Africa. The next day she called and said, "Yes, I'll go with you, but not because my girls are OK with it. A couple of months ago my pastor stopped me in the aisle at church and said, 'Barb, you're going to Africa.' I had never even had a desire to go to Africa, so when you called, I realized it was of the Lord. Yes, I'll go."

A month later we were on our way to Nairobi, where we stayed with our dear friend, Sharon Higgins (now Hester), who was ministering at New Life Home for abandoned and orphaned babies.

Barb and I began looking at big houses, thinking we would rent. But all the owners refused us, not wanting a lot of children in their homes. We looked at so many places and felt so frustrated because time was going by and nothing seemed to be happening for us.

One day while shopping in a big mall (yes, Nairobi has several big malls), we noticed a real estate office with pictures of homes and properties for sale and for rent. One of those pictures looked so familiar that I went in and asked about that home. I couldn't believe it when I was told where it was and that it was for sale. It had previously housed a Bible School where Paul had taught and where we had visited many times. The school had been offered the opportunity to buy the property, but they didn't have the money. It was then sold to a businessman, who, after living there two years, was transferred to Kampala, Uganda, so he put it up for sale. We went out the next day, looked it over and said, "THIS IS IT!" When Paul arrived in Kenya a couple of weeks later we met with the owners. They agreed on our price, and we said we'd take it. In Kenya, when you buy property, they give you three months to get your money together, but we felt to ask them for six months. We gave them $25,000 and they agreed to give us six months.

We returned home to America. While in prayer one morning, the Lord spoke to me again, saying, "You asked for six months to raise the money because you thought I couldn't do it in three, right?"

Well of course He was right. I was ashamed and asked Him to forgive me for my unbelief. It was wonderful the way God began to pour money into our hands. Every place we went, showing a DVD of the land, people gave money to help buy the property. When we arrived at Faith Temple in Rochester, New York for their midweek service, we were excited about what God was doing. After the service we went out to eat with Pastor Mary and Pastors Steve and Darla Edlin, who asked us how much money we had received so far. We figured it up and saw that we were down to $70,000. Paul was scheduled to speak at another church in Rochester on Sunday, so they asked us to stop by their office on Monday before leaving town and they would give us a check, not mentioning the amount.

Monday came, and we met them at the church office where they handed us a check. To our total shock it was for $70,000.00! AWESOME hardly describes how we felt! But even more awesome was this: The day before we received the check was exactly one month from the day we signed the papers for the property! God didn't need six months... He didn't need three months... He provided the money in one month to the day! He wants to bless us so much when we are obedient, even when we are seventy-five years old. God does things in His timing.

We sent the money to Jon and Molly (our son and his wife who were missionaries in Kenya) and started planning what to build. When you have been in the ministry for many years you make lots of friends all over the country. Bill and Ruth Defibaugh were pastoring in Bedford, Pennsylvania; Bill was also an architect, building churches. Paul called him and asked if he would like to go to Nairobi and plan how to lay out the building or buildings. Bill drew plans for enlarging the existing house for Jon and Molly and their family to live in, and a small house for us and then an orphanage—how big, what kind, etc. While there they met a wonderful Christian builder and his architect who agreed to work with us.

KKV Compound

Paul and I returned home, and the first thing we did was to put our house up for sale. It sold for our asking price in one day for cash. Think God was in it? We packed up our furniture and other things into a container, sent it to Nairobi, and moved out, staying in a rented apartment near the land to watch the buildings go up. Jon and Molly were on board with us and were wanting to be a part of this vision so they moved into the house after it was enlarged and we moved into our little house shortly after it was built. Now it was time to see the orphanage built.

Kings Kids Village - Faith House

The building they designed was a four apartment building rather than individual houses, to save room for more buildings. It would have four apartments, each one housing ten kids so siblings could stay together, with a set of parents to oversee them.

Faith House

It was exciting to see it go up. The a m a z i n g thing is that every time the builder would come asking for money to pay his workers or for material, it was always there. When it was finished, we named it FAITH HOUSE, in honor of Faith Temple.

Before telling you about our great dedication day, let me tell you about the name we chose to call our whole five acres.

We were visiting a church in Picayune, Mississippi before moving to Kenya. We had shared with them the vision for the orphanage. That night a dear elder in the church couldn't sleep so he began to pray for us. God gave him a vision. He saw us sitting in a wagon at the top of a hill, ready to go down. People were saying, "The Sterns are on the downhill side of their ministry after many years of service." He saw

Paul let go of the brake, and as we drove down the hill people began to

throw things into our wagon, so by the time we got to the bottom, our wagon was full. God spoke to his heart, "Many shall grow up to become pastors, teachers, doctors, and leaders in their country, for out of the forgotten shall come the begotten." Who are the begotten? Children of the King of Kings. So the name, KINGS KIDS VILLAGE came to be, and we think it is very fitting.

Dedication day finally came in May 2004. What a celebration we had! All our children came out and some of our grand children as well. We had our first two orphans already, Wally (or as he now calls himself Walter) and Julien, children rescued by New Life Home. And we had our first set of parents, Pastors Zedi and Mary, who had just been replaced in their church by a younger pastor, so they were free to come and be Mama and Papa for a household of kids. People came from around the neighborhood and from Nairobi Lighthouse Church. All wanted to see Faith

House. Pastor Don Matheny prayed the prayer of dedication, and the presence of the Lord was awesome! And, everything was paid for!

Soon other children were made known to Jon and Molly—children with no one to care for them or with grandmas too old to provide for them. I cannot begin to tell you some of the horror stories of where these children came from, but I can tell

Kings Kids

you that they found physical, social, psychological, and most of all, spiritual shelter at Kings Kids Village (KKV). They are LOVED! Gradually the building began to fill up as people began to hear about KKV.

Paul and I came back to the United States soon after that, as he was experiencing some physical problems. However, we went back to Nairobi in December of 2008 for a couple of months to see how everything was going. One evening, while attending a week of special prayer at Nairobi Lighthouse Church, the church our kids called their church, I was surprised when Jon said we were taking two vans because a number of the children (not the little ones) wanted to go as well.

During the worship time, I could hear the voices of the people behind me, praising the Lord and singing with great joy. I turned around to look and saw that it was three of our young teenage boys from KKV. Their eyes were closed, their hands were raised, and they were totally absorbed in worshiping the Lord. I said to God, "It's worth everything just to see these kids loving God like they do."

Loving the KKV Kids

CHAPTER FIVE

The Vision Grows

So, let me bring you up to date. The orphanage is full, and some of the original kids have already ventured out on their own. Although the Kenyan government allows us to release them at age eighteen, we see to it they have a job, or college, whichever they are suited for.

Three of our young men live in an apartment which we furnish and give them an allowance for food, but they attend high school every day, as they had a very late beginning in school before coming to KKV.

Our eldest girl, Essie, is just finishing Nursing School. She is very involved in the church where I saw her one day, serving the pastors between services. The pastor's wife, Amy Matheny told me this: "If Essie were the only child you brought through KKV, it would have been worth all you spent; she is such a blessing."

Some of our children, of course, are still very young or have never been to school, but with the wonderful teachers we have they'll catch up. Which reminds me to tell you about our great school. Molly's dad and mom, Dr Bill and Mary Hensold, have been very involved in KKV. Mary wanted to see a school built but she became ill and passed away before she could. Dr. Bill Hensold, asked people to give money for the school instead of bringing flowers to Mary's funeral, which they did. It wasn't long until there stood an awesome school—three buildings. Two other orphanages send their high school kids there also, so it is full.

Playground

Let me tell you about the parents God has given us. I told you about Pastors Zedi and Mary, now let me tell you about Joshua and Crystobel, long time friends of Jon and Molly. One day Joshua and Crystobel came to visit; Jon and Molly were totally surprised when Joshua said they had come to help.

"What can we do?" they asked. Jon replied, "Well, we need another set of parents." He didn't really think they would take him up on it as Joshua is a professor at a Christian University in Nairobi. But to his surprise, Joshua said, "When do you want us to come? We're free now as our youngest child just started University and has a place to live." Joshua then told Jon and Molly that a number of years ago he had walked by the land we now call KKV and God told him that he would one day be living there. So, now was the time. They came, and what a blessing they are. Now there is a Papa in one of the downstairs apartments and one upstairs, so even the kids who don't have a Papa living in their apartment feel like he is their Papa. This Papa goes to work every day, just like other Papas do, giving the kids an example of how life can and should be.

Two Mamas have an auntie helping them; Tabitha, an awesome lady, and Florence, who also loves the kids dearly.

With Molly Stern

Eleanor at her computer

Eleanor at the Keyboard

CHAPTER SIX

Challenge to Fulfill Your Vision or Calling

So now are we done? No, no, no! There are more than one million orphans just in Kenya. We have faith for the ability and space to take on more than the fifty at KKV. We hope to buy a beautiful five acre plot next door. It has a building on it that can accommodate many more children.

I am now eighty-eight years old. The Lord took Paul to his heavenly home February 19, 2013. God has my days numbered, as He does yours and I will work until I am no longer able. I can't do as much physically as I did a few years ago, but my fingers still hit the keys both on my computer and on my piano. My mind is still working, and most of all, the Holy Sprit of God is in me to fulfill all He has planned for me in my lifetime here on earth.

Don't think there is nothing you can do because you're too old. Don't THINK with your AGE, THINK with your HEART.

> Even in old age they will
> still produce fruit; they will
> remain vital and green.
> (Psalm 92:14)

What a promise! So, pour out your heart to Him and ask Him, "What would you like me to do?" He has unusual ways of showing us where we fit and how we can be a blessing, no matter what our age. Remember, GROWING OLD IS MANDATORY—GROWING UP IS OPTIONAL. And here's another great quote from a great world leader, Winston Churchill:

> "We make a LIVING by what we get; we make a LIFE by what we give."

There is always something you can do to take you out of yourself and into what God has planned for you. Who knows, you might live to be a hundred; and when you get to heaven, God will welcome you home with,

> "WELL DONE, GOOD AND FAITHFUL SERVANT;... BECAUSE YOU WERE FAITHFUL IN A VERY LITTLE, HAVE AUTHORITY OVER TEN CITIES." (Matthew 25:23a; Luke 19:17b NKJV)

Our reward will be in heaven, as we just do all that God enables us to do here on earth. That's what counts above all! So, keep on keeping on.

YOU'RE NEVER TOO OLD

And my life's story is not finished yet!

Paul Stern Praying for Orphans

Made in the USA
Lexington, KY
10 July 2015